To:

....

From:

....

Date:

....

PRAYERS THAT HEAL

Faith-Building Prayers

When You Need a Miracle

REGINALD CHERRY, M.D.

THOMAS NELSON PUBLISHERS®
Nashville

Published in Nashville, Tennessee, by Thomas Nelson, Inc.

Scripture quotations are from the King James Version of the Bible.

Cover and interior design: Uttley/DouPonce DesignWorks, www.uddesignworks.com

Library of Congress Cataloging-in-Publication Data

Cherry, Reginald B.
   Prayers that heal : faith-building prayers when you need a miracle / Reginald Cherry.
      p. cm.
   ISBN 0-7852-6825-1 (hc)
   1. Sick—Prayer-books and devotions—English. I. Title.

BV270.C48 2001
242'.861—dc21   00-046569
                                                                              CIP

Printed in the United States of America.
1 2 3 4 5 6 — 06 05 04 03 02 01

This book is dedicated to the
important people who have changed my life:
my wife, Linda,
my precious children, DeAnna and Scott;
and most of all, Jesus,
who called me out of darkness into
His marvelous light.

CONTENTS

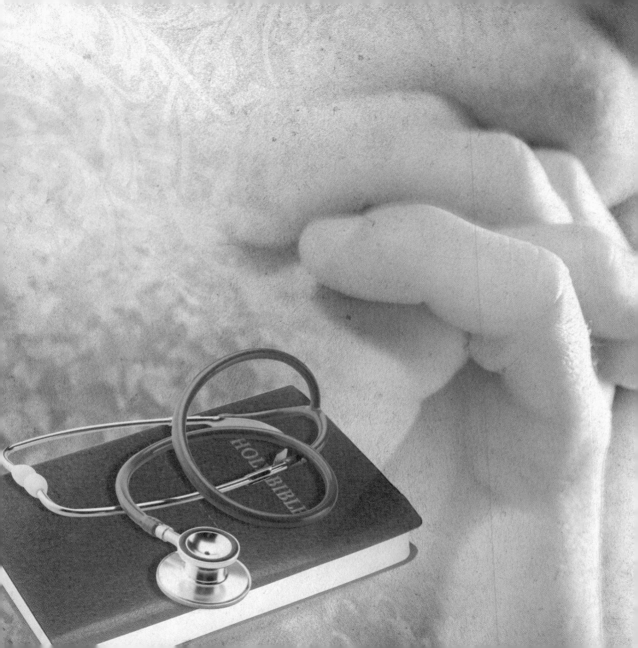

INTRODUCTION

I will pray with the spirit,
and I will pray with the understanding also.

— 1 CORINTHIANS 14:15

T he prayers shared in this book are actual prayers I have prayed with my patients for several years. Prayer changes things. I have seen patients healed of nearly every conceivable disease. There is no case too hard for God.

These are not intended to be rote prayers, but intended, rather, to share with you "effectual fervent" prayers, as mentioned in James 5:16. This type of prayer "availeth much," as James said.

The disciples in Luke 11:1 asked Jesus to teach them how to pray, and Jesus then gave them what we have come to know as the Lord's Prayer. We want to share with you "prayers that heal."

Praying with understanding about a specific disease (1 Cor. 14:15) enables you to pray a strong, fervent, effectual prayer. We understand what the attack of the enemy is against our body and speak to the specific mountain according to what Jesus declared: "Whosoever shall say unto this mountain, Be thou removed, and be thou cast into the sea; and shall not doubt in his heart, but shall believe that those things which he saith shall come to pass; he shall have whatsoever he saith" (Mark 11:23).

In these pages, we walk with you as you face various diseases. Obtain all the information you can about the disease. Find out what you can do in the natural and combine this information with your faith in God's Word. We believe with you, in Jesus' name, that your prayers will "availeth much."

In His name,

REGINALD B. CHERRY, M.D.

PRAYERS
THAT HEAL

DIABETES

Diabetes has become an extremely common and devastating disease. As many as 16 million Americans are affected by diabetes, and there are nearly 800,000 new cases each year. It is the leading cause of blindness in persons under the age of sixty-five, as well as the leading cause of renal disease (kidney failure) and surgery, such as limb amputations. It increases the risk of heart disease, stroke, and blockage in the more distant vessels by a factor of two to seven (as compared with the risk for a nondiabetic).

Diabetes is a disease in which the body does not produce or properly use insulin. Insulin is a hormone that our bodies need to convert sugar, starches, and other foods into energy. It is necessary for us to understand how the enemy uses diabetes to attack our earthen vessels. Understanding how diabetes attacks our bodies enables us to pray fervently and effectually.

By far, the most common type of diabetes is known as Type II, which represents 90 to 95 percent of the diabetic population. We must direct our prayers specifically at the source of the attack in diabetes; this is the mountain that we must speak to for God to remove.

Speak to insulin resistance. It seems that the primary problem is an insulin resistance in the various tissues. Insulin, secreted by the beta cells of the pancreas, has to work on various receptors in other areas of the body to allow glucose to enter the cells and provide energy. In Type II diabetes there is a resistance to the action of diabetes on the receptors and the glucose is not allowed to enter the cells; this in turn causes the blood sugar to rise.

Break the generational curse. Diabetes often goes on for years before it is actually diagnosed. If diabetes runs in your family, you need to break the generational curse (Deut. 5:9).

Speak to the receptors. Also speak to the receptors in your body to be sensitive to the action of insulin. After several years, the beta cells of the pancreas, which try to produce more insulin to overcome this resistance, in a sense "wear out."

So if you have been diagnosed with diabetes, you should consider two different avenues of prayer:

1. *Pray for an increased sensitivity of the receptor cells* to allow insulin to enter the cells and provide energy.
2. *Speak to the beta cells in the pancreas* to produce adequate amounts of insulin.

A Prayer for Healing of Diabetes

Father, in the name of Jesus, I speak to the receptor cells in my body. I command them to become more sensitive and less resistant to the effects of insulin, allowing glucose to enter my body cells, supply energy, and perform all the functions You designed.

In Jesus' name, I speak to the beta cells of my pancreas and command them to secrete adequate and normal amounts of insulin. I believe, Father, that my blood sugar levels will drop, and my arteries, nerves, and eyes will be protected from destruction caused by high blood sugar levels.

Father, I ask You to help me do my part by maintaining my normal weight and eating the proper foods as I avoid simple carbohydrates and increase the fiber content of my diet.

Father, reveal to me all of the things in the natural that I can do, such as taking supplements and eating the right foods to take care of this temple. As I do those things I can do in the natural, I will believe and look to You to perform the supernatural in protecting all parts of my body from the effects of diabetes as my insulin levels become normal and my blood sugar levels drop.

Thank You, Lord God, that I was healed of this disease by the blood of Jesus two thousand years ago, and therefore I am praying for the full manifestation of total healing in my body because by His stripes I was healed (1 Peter 2:24). In Jesus' name, I pray. Amen.

ARTHRITIS

A rthritis is one of the most common, annoying, aggravating, and painful problems faced by men and women as they get older. The good news is, though, that we do not have to *suffer* from the degeneration in the cartilage of our joints. We all may have some degree of change in the joints on X ray, for example, but this is irrelevant if we can move the joint and be free of pain and do the things God has called us to do without painful symptoms.

In the natural, there are many things that are beneficial to the joint. Glucosamine 500 mg three times daily has been shown to be as effective as prescription medicine for osteoarthritis (the most common form of arthritis). This natural substance is produced in the body and stimulates the repair of cartilage while reducing inflammation in the joints. It often takes two to three months before the beneficial effects occur, but this, combined with the power of prayer, has actually prevented some of our patients from having to undergo joint replacement surgery. Another useful natural substance is chondroitin sulfate, which is also produced in the body and helps make the cartilage that lines joints more elastic by causing increased water retention. It can also block enzymes that tend to destroy cartilage. A typical dose would be 1,000 to 2,000 mg daily. Both of these substances are natural, very safe, and available at health food stores.

We encourage our patients not to look solely to natural means for their healing, but to combine the natural substances (that is, the things that they can do) with their supernatural power of faith and the power of prayer in order to see the manifestation of their healing.

There are dozens of forms of arthritis, but the two most common are *osteoarthritis,* which is the "wear and tear kind of arthritis," and *rheumatoid arthritis,* which is due to an immune system reaction that attacks the lining of joints. If you are suffering from arthritis, combine the power of natural substances with the supernatural power of prayer.

I want to share with you a prayer that you might find helpful in praying for this problem. Remember that the disciples asked Jesus to "teach us how to pray." You will find listed below a typical prayer that we might pray with our patients.

A Prayer for Healing of Arthritis

Father, I come before You in the name of Your precious Son, Jesus, thanking You that Jesus bore in His own body two thousand years ago the symptoms of the infirmity of arthritis. I thank You that because He bore this disease in His own body, I was healed! Therefore,

Father, I am coming before You to seek the manifestation of that healing in my physical body. In the name of Jesus, I speak to the cartilage in my joints [name the joint where you are suffering pain], and I command that cartilage to increase in thickness and become more pliable and more elastic. I further pray that the inflammatory cells that lead to swelling and pain be removed from that joint. I say in Jesus' name that I will be able to move that joint and serve You day to day without pain, symptoms, or inflammation. Father, as I do all I can do in the natural, I look to You to do the supernatural that I cannot do. I send forth the healing, anointing power of the Holy Spirit, the Comforter, who resides within me into my body and into my joints, and I speak comfort and healing to these joints. Thank You, Father, that my manifestation of healing is on the way. I praise You, Father, that You are revealing the specific pathway that I need to walk that will lead to my healing. I thank You for all of these things in the precious name of Jesus, and I close this prayer praising You and thanking You because through my eye of faith, I see myself healed. In Jesus' name, amen.

CANCER

There are many different kinds of cancer that attack the human body, but cancers in general share certain characteristics. Cancer basically represents a failure of the body's immune system with a weakening in T cells, B cells, and natural killer cells that are designed to recognize and attack abnormally dividing cancer cells.

Cancer tends to create its own system of blood vessels (angiogenesis) to supply the increased amount of blood needed to sustain tumor growth. By understanding some of these processes contributing to cancer growth, we can pray specifically and effectually. On the natural side, God has provided substances from His creation that both strengthen our immune systems (glutathione, selenium, vitamin E, coenzyme Q_{10}, zinc, B vitamins) and actually kill abnormal cancer cells (catechins from green tea extract, sulforophane from broccoli, lycopene). We should seek God in prayer as to what He would have us do in the natural as we also seek Him in faith to do the supernatural.

A PRAYER FOR HEALING OF CANCER

Father, I thank You that through the name of Jesus, You have given me authority over the works of darkness that would attack my body. I therefore speak to cancer and command it to cease in my body. I speak specifically to my immune system and command the T cells and other components to be activated and to rise up against abnormal cancer cells. I command the cancer's blood supply to wither and die and for the abnormal cancer cell divisions to stop. I ask You, Father, to reveal to me those natural substances you would have me use to strengthen my immune system. I ask You to also reveal those herbal substances and extracts You would have me use to kill and overcome cancer cells in my body. As I do what I can and know to do in the natural, I look to You, Father, to touch my body supernaturally, and I thank You that by the stripes of Your Son, Jesus, I was healed and my manifestation of healing is on the way. In Jesus' name, I thank You for my healing. Amen.

DEPRESSION

Depression is a devastating attack against the human mind, and studies show that up to 25 percent of the population suffer depression at any given time! We know that depression (and all disease) is an attack from the world of darkness originating from the evil one. We often allow depression to occur, however, with very little help from the enemy simply because we do not follow God's Word and apply Scriptures such as 1 Peter 5:7, where we are instructed to cast our care on Him.

Carrying worry, anxiety, and anger as well as not dealing with losses in our lives can result in physical changes in our bodies. Chemicals that conduct various nerve impulses throughout the brain, known as neurotransmitters, affect our thoughts, moods, and emotions. With depression, these chemicals (serotonin, dopamine, norepinephrine, monoamine oxidase, and others) become depleted, and this depletion can become so severe that it makes it difficult for us to even read and receive the Word of God into our lives. God has provided various things for us to do in the natural (such as using St. John's wort, kava, valerian, and other substances) to help restore these chemical levels to normal as we begin applying the Word of God and prayer in the supernatural realm. As the blind man in John 9:7 was healed as he "went his way," we, too, must find our own unique pathway that will lead to healing of depression. It often involves a combination of natural substances along with our faith in God's Word and our applying God's Word through prayer as we speak to the mountain called depression.

Here is a way we often pray with patients who are seeking healing from depression.

A PRAYER FOR HEALING OF DEPRESSION

Thank You, Father, that I can come into Your presence in the name of Your precious Son, Jesus. I thank You, Father, that Jesus bore in His body all of my infirmities and all of my iniquities, including the depression that I am experiencing. Since I was healed of this according to 1 Peter 2:24, I therefore seek You for the unique pathway that will lead to the total and complete manifestation of my healing. Through the Holy Spirit, Father, reveal to me all the things I can do in the natural to overcome this attack, and as I do all I can do, Lord, I look to You to do the supernatural that I cannot do. I speak to the neurotransmitter chemicals in my brain and I command them to be normal in the name of Jesus. I thank You, Father, that I have the mind of Christ and that my thoughts will be clear and all symptoms of depression will go. I cast my cares and worries upon You according to 1 Peter 5:7. I call myself healed and, through my eye of faith, I see myself healed and I believe that the full manifestation of my healing is on the way. I believe, Father, that You will satisfy me with long life and fulfill the number of my days. I thank You that I have authority over the powers of darkness, and in Jesus' name I execute that authority and command the grip of darkness to be released from my mind. Thank You, Father, that it is done, and as I am set free of this depression, I will find, follow, and complete Your divine will for my life. In Jesus' name I pray, amen.

HEART DISEASE

Cardiovascular disease, which includes heart attack, stroke, and hardening of the arteries, kills more people than all forms of cancer combined. Heart disease was on the decrease for several years but has now begun to increase again. As a result of hardening of the artery walls, the artery becomes stiffer, which can lead to high blood pressure. The effects of this can, in turn, lead to kidney problems, heart enlargement, and stroke as well.

Though there are many factors that interact to cause heart disease and hardening of the arteries, the most common and most basic underlying problem is the formation of a cholesterol plaque on the artery walls, which causes a disruption in the normal blood flow. These plaques can rupture and allow a blood clot to form, which disrupts the flow of blood through the vessel, often leading to a heart attack or stroke.

In order to pray with understanding we have to be able to speak to these specific processes such as plaque formation, cholesterol deposits, and blood clot formation. The more specifically we speak to the mountain and take authority over it, the more effective our prayer. It would be wise for all of us to speak to our arteries and bind the formation of blood clots, whether we have been diagnosed with heart disease or not. The Bible tells us that the life of the flesh is in the blood (Lev. 17:11). It is the strategy of the enemy to obstruct blood flow, and this leads to major health problems.

A Prayer for Healing of Heart Disease

Father, in the name of Jesus I thank You for healthy arteries and blood vessels. I know according to Your Word that the life of the flesh is in the blood. I therefore speak to the walls and linings of all my arteries according to Mark 11:23. I command any plaque formation to disappear in the name of Jesus. I further pray in the name of Jesus that there will be no clot formation that would obstruct these blood vessels. I pray specifically that the platelets in my bloodstream will function normally and in a manner that will not cause a clot to block the normal flow of blood. I thank You, Father, for revelation knowledge of the things I can do in the natural to reverse any cholesterol plaque that has formed and prevent any plaque from forming in the future. Reveal to me, Lord, those specific vitamins, minerals, supplements, herbs, and whatever other natural chemicals I should be using to protect my blood vessels and vital organs and reverse any damage that has already occurred. I thank You, Father, that my coronary arteries will supply blood to my heart muscle as You designed them to do. I pray that my carotid arteries and all of the cerebral arteries supplying blood to my brain will remain free of blockage and free of blood clots. Thank You that my kidneys will function normally and the circulation throughout all of my extremities will be normal. I thank You, Father, that Your Son, Jesus, bore in His own body on the cross all artery problems that I might ever face and by His stripes I was healed two thousand years ago. I will endeavor to do all that I can and all that I know to do to protect my arteries and my vascular system. I will trust You, Father, to do the supernatural that I cannot do as my greatest and fondest desire is to finish the course on this earth that You have called me to finish and to finish it with joy. In Jesus' name, amen.

EYE PROBLEMS

Many of us are aware of natural ways to take care of our eyesight, but we need to formulate our knowledge into a specific prayer. We must never lose sight of the fact that God's pathway to healing often involves the supernatural touch of God as our faith gives substance to those things hoped for. Prayer is a supernatural way we touch God and change circumstances around us. However, frequently the pathway of healing is a combination of the supernatural and the natural.

Cataracts, a clouding of the lens of the eyes, for example, are the leading cause of blindness worldwide. Vitamin E, vitamin C, alpha-lipoic acid, selenium, and glutathione are all useful in cataract prevention (and perhaps even reversal). A second major eye disease, macular degeneration, results from pigment loss in the retina, leading to eventual loss of central vision. The supplements lutein and zeaxanthin can actually restore this pigment loss.

So many Christians have been attacked with the problem of cataracts, loss of night vision, macular degeneration, glaucoma, and other diseases that we must be on guard to protect our bodies in this area. Here is a prayer that will be helpful to you as you come before the throne of God seeking your healing from eye problems.

A Prayer for Healing
and Protection from Eye Problems

Father, as I come before You in the name of Your precious Son, Jesus, I thank You for the divine health that He purchased for me on Calvary. I thank You, Father, that Jesus gave us the authority of His name and the anointing of the Holy Spirit to overcome the works of the enemy that attack my body. Father, I thank You specifically for sharp eyesight and clear vision. I thank You, Father, for protecting the lens of my eye from cataracts. I speak to any cloudiness in the lens and command it to go in Jesus' name. I command nutrients and antioxidants and protective chemicals in my blood to flow in and touch the lens of my eye and protect it from degenerative changes. As I place these nutrients into my body, I thank You, Father, that they will go forth and accomplish the purpose for which You created them. I further thank You, Father, that the pressure within my eye will be normal, and glaucoma will not be allowed to exist within my eye and cause damage. I will do my part, Father, in Jesus' name by taking in the nutrients from Your plant kingdom that will help protect my eye from the effects of abnormal pressure, and I thank You that damage will not occur to my optic nerve. I thank You, Father, that I will continue to have sharp, clear vision and will not suffer the effects of macular degeneration. I speak to the pigments that You created in the area of my retina and I command them to increase.

Thank You, Father, that my vision will be sharp and focused. I will eat those substances and take in those nutrients that will protect the macular area of my retina, and I thank You, Father, that dimmed vision and blindness will not exist in this temple. I praise You and thank You, Father, in the name of Jesus, for Your marvelous revelations about how You created this temple and for the provision that You have given me in the form of natural substances. I will use those natural substances to do my part to protect my temple and keep my vision sharp as I finish the race that You have called me to finish on this earth. I thank You, Lord, that I will be satisfied with long life according to Psalm 91. In Jesus' name, I praise You for all of these things. Amen.

HYPOGLYCEMIA

Hypoglycemia is a term describing low blood sugar (as opposed to hyperglycemia, which is high blood sugar or diabetes). Weakness and fatigue are very common with low blood sugar, and some patients experience sweating, faintness, a drop in blood pressure, and an increase in heart rate during periods of actual hypoglycemia.

What happens in the human body after the consumption of certain foods, particularly refined sugars and other foods with what is known as a high "glycemic index," is that the sugar or glucose level in the blood rises rapidly. This causes the beta cells of the pancreas to secrete large amounts of insulin to lower the sugar levels. Many times the sudden outpouring of insulin is too much and causes the blood sugar level to drop below normal levels.

Technically doctors diagnose hypoglycemia when fasting blood sugar levels are under 65 as measured by a blood test or under 65 on a glucose tolerance test. We have some patients, however, who have had fasting blood sugar levels as low as 40 and feel no symptoms at all. The best way to accurately diagnose hypoglycemia is with a glucose tolerance test where a person is given a measured amount of sugar (typically 75 grams) and regular hourly blood samples are taken for five hours. When we do these tests, we also record heart rate and blood pressure each time we take a one-hour blood specimen. To enhance the accuracy, insulin levels can also be done at the same time the sugar levels are performed.

We have found that many times when patients experience symptoms of weakness, fatigue, dizziness, and light-headedness after meals, they are not experiencing actual low blood sugar or hypoglycemia. Instead they are responding to the rapid drop in the sugar level even though this drop may be within the range of normal. The basic underlying problem, whether it's the rapid drop in sugar or very low sugar levels, is usually caused by simple carbohydrates (sugars) as well as certain starches (potatoes, for example). Because of limited fiber intake with our food, sugars are absorbed very rapidly, causing the fluctuations in blood sugar. Remember that many vegetables contain natural sugars and starches, including potatoes, carrots, and others.

Fruits contain the natural sugar fructose, but most fruits have a high fiber intake. You are wondering, "What does fiber have to do with my sugar level?" Well, God's design was to have us ingest fiber along with the carrots and natural fruit sugars. The fiber slows the absorption of the sugar and causes it to be absorbed into the bloodstream in a slow, steady manner that prevents rapid fluctuations in insulin and the subsequent rise and fall in the sugar levels.

Many of the currently popular diets recommend low carbohydrates and eliminate foods such as baked potatoes and carrots to avoid the rapid absorption of sugar and the increases in insulin levels. The solution, however, is not to avoid these but to simply combine them with higher fiber. For example, if you consumed pinto beans with carrots as part of your meal, the soluble fiber in the beans would prevent the rapid rise in blood sugar due to the carrots and avoid the insulin fluctuations. Thick dark breads (with the grains visible) will accomplish the same thing. Ezekiel bread, mentioned in the Bible (Ezek. 4:9) and now commercially available, will also help regulate blood sugar levels.

Rapidly fluctuating sugar levels and low sugar levels (hypoglycemia) can indeed make you feel bad. When sugar levels get too low or begin dropping, some folks will consume additional sugar, which temporarily corrects the problem but only sets up a vicious cycle of ups and downs in the blood glucose levels. This is not the answer. The answer involves avoiding or limiting refined sugar and consuming fiber with those foods that are high in natural sugars. Increases in insulin levels contribute to obesity, and thus we need to understand how God designed our bodies to take in fiber along with our normal daily intake.

A Prayer for Healing of Hypoglycemia

Father, in the name of Jesus, I thank You that my pancreas is functioning normally. I thank You that my blood sugar levels will not drop too low, and as I consume increased amounts of fiber in my diet, the natural sugar that I do consume will be absorbed slowly and evenly, causing my insulin levels to change within a normal range. I stand against all symptoms of fatigue, tiredness, dizziness, light-headedness, and drops in blood pressure that may be caused by rapid drops in my blood sugar or low blood sugar. As I do things in the natural, nutritionally, to guard the secretion of insulin in my body, I thank You that You will supernaturally regulate the beta cells of my pancreas to produce normal amounts of insulin and that I will not experience any symptoms associated with low blood sugar. Thank You, Father, for guarding and protecting this temple and giving me Your wisdom of its wonderful design. In Jesus' name I pray, amen.

IMMUNE SYSTEM PROBLEMS

G od created our immune systems as a natural hedge of protection. A strong immune system protects us from illnesses ranging from bacterial and viral infections to cancer.

I don't need to tell you that we live in an evil world—evil in both the spiritual and natural realms. We face constant bombardment on the natural side from various viral and bacterial agents that not only cause infection, but also may be the root cause of diseases such as chronic fatigue syndrome, and more.

We hear stories of flesh-eating bacteria. We are now discovering that foreign bacterial invaders may contribute to hardening of the arteries and heart attacks. Even the bacteria residing in our mouths can enter our bloodstream and possibly cause problems with our heart.

Abnormal cell divisions occur almost weekly in our bodies. These can develop into cancer if left unchecked by a strong immune system. God does not want us to have to constantly dwell on these potential problems or live in fear of them.

As His children, we dwell under His hand of protection, but He also created a hedge of protection known as our immune system. Various components of this system, such as macrophages, B lymphocytes, T cells, and natural killer cells, are standing by ready to protect us on a moment's notice.

What we put into our temples and how we protect them can enhance the function or weaken the ability of the immune system to protect us. Natural supplements such as glutathione, selenium, coenzyme Q_{10}, yogurt, zinc, B vitamins, and vitamin E all strengthen as well as balance our immune systems. The wonderful thing is that they all originate from God's natural creation. We all need to pray specifically for a strong immune system.

A Prayer for a Strong Immune System

Father, I thank You for Your hand of protection that rests over me. I thank You also for the natural protection You created in my body in the form of an immune system. I therefore speak specifically to the lymphocytes and command them in Jesus' name to become activated and balanced. I speak to the T cells, the B cells, the macrophage cells, and the natural killer cells and command them to function strongly and in the balance that You created them. I thank You, Father, that as I supplement my temple with various natural substances such as glutathione, selenium, coenzyme Q_{10}, yogurt, zinc, B vitamins, and vitamin E that Your anointing will flow through these natural substances to strengthen *and balance my immune system. Thank You that my immune system will instantly recognize and overcome any foreign invader or any process that occurs in my body that does not line up with Your Word. I further thank You, Lord, that my immune system will maintain the proper balance and not become overactivated as a result of fighting off foreign invaders and substances. I will walk in Your divine protection, Father, doing all I can in the natural to enhance this incredible immune system. I will trust You to provide the supernatural protection that I cannot. I thank You for all of these things, Father, and I give You all of the glory. In the precious name of Jesus, amen.*

HARDENING
OF THE ARTERIES

Next to cancer, hardening of the arteries is one of the biggest concerns facing us today. This disease (also known as *atherosclerosis*) is, in fact, the leading cause of heart attacks and strokes, which kill more people in industrialized countries than all the forms of cancer combined.

Is there anything we can do to stop this process? Yes, there are multiple things you can do to avoid having to face this ravaging problem. Read on.

Scientists are finding that hardening of the arteries is really an inflammation in the arteries. Most of us think that hardening of the arteries is just a condition in which solid calcium deposits form in the arteries as calcium forms in the water pipes in our homes. This is really not accurate.

The bad LDL cholesterol forms a solid or semisolid plaque or deposit that can stiffen artery walls. This plaque consists of white blood cells, smooth muscle cells, platelets, and other components, but it basically represents an inflammatory process in the plaque.

Amazingly, half of the people with these plaques, which can clog the arteries, have normal cholesterol levels. It is the initial damage to the artery lining caused by the bad cholesterol that sets the stage for inflammation. This is why taking one low-dose (81 mg) "enteric-coated" baby aspirin per day can work wonders in preventing heart disease—it stops the inflammation. (The term "enteric-coated" will appear on the label.) Interestingly, regular aspirin (325 mg) is not as effective as the lower-dose 81 mg aspirin.

Why does the cholesterol damage the arteries? It is the oxidation or breakdown of the LDL cholesterol that enables it to harm the healthy cells lining the arteries. This is why it is so critical to provide an "antioxidant" in the form of vitamin E (800 IU daily), vitamin C (2,000 mg daily), selenium (200 mcg daily), and other antioxidants such as the carotenes, coenzyme Q_{10}, etc.

Protein is another potential culprit. It is not the protein we eat (which is good for us), but the breakdown of certain types of protein (amino acids) into a by-product known as homocystine that can cause problems. High homocystine levels can damage the arteries, and these levels increase when we lack sufficient amounts of B vitamins in our diet. To prevent hardening of the arteries, we recommend folic acid (600 mcg daily), B_6 (75 mg daily), and B_{12} (100 mcg daily). These amounts of B vitamins keep the homocystine levels low and thus offer significant protection from hardening of the arteries.

Cholesterol levels can be reduced. We need to get the LDL (bad cholesterol) level under 100, and the HDL (good cholesterol) level above 40 to 45. Please, please don't take the attitude that hardening of the arteries will not happen to you. Rather, use your endeavors to heal yourself as the Amplified Bible exhorts in Proverbs 18:9. These points are critical in protecting you from heart disease and stroke.

You must ask yourself the question "Will I do something simple to protect my body?" Of course you will, and God is making it simple for all of us to finish our course with joy and not face the common diseases the world faces.

A Prayer for Protection
from Hardening of the Arteries

Father, I thank You in the name of Jesus that my arteries will remain open, my blood flow will remain normal, and my artery walls will not thicken or stiffen. I thank You, Father, that the "life of the flesh is in the blood" according to Leviticus 17:11 and that life will continue to flow to every cell in my body. I thank You, Father, that the bad cholesterol levels will not deposit on the artery walls. I thank You that blood clots will not form on my artery walls, blocking the flow of life through my vessels. Father, I thank You for giving me wisdom to do what I can do to protect this temple from artery blockage and hardening of the arteries. Quicken to me whether I should be on low-dose aspirin to prevent inflammation and blood clots. Guide me as to supplementing my diet with additional forms of vitamins E and C and other supplements that You created in Your awesome plant kingdom. As I supplement my body, I give You thanks that harmful chemical substances will not form in my vessels. I further thank You, Lord, that my cholesterol levels will be normal. I thank You, Father, for providing certain medications that can lower my cholesterol, though I pray that I can do this naturally with diet and supplements as You guide me. However, if one of the new cholesterol-lowering medications is to be used in my pathway to healing, Father, I will be obedient and follow the leading of the Holy Spirit. I know that if the Holy Spirit gives this instruction and direction, I will suffer no side effects from the medication. Thank You, Father, for setting me free of any generational curses of hardening of the arteries. I thank You, Father, that I will fulfill the number of my days according to Your promises. In Jesus' name, I pray. Amen.

HEADACHES

There are several different kinds of headaches, each of which requires a slightly different way of praying and different natural treatments. Headaches should not be a source of fear, as God did not give us a spirit of fear but of power, love, and a sound mind (2 Tim. 1:7).

On the other hand, certain warning signs—such as the sudden onset of a headache in a person who has never had a headache before or steadily increasing headaches with changes in vision—should be evaluated to be sure the headache is properly diagnosed and treated.

A majority of headaches fall into the following classes: tension headaches, migraine headaches, combination headaches, cluster headaches, and simple headaches. Physicians typically treat these types of headaches with various prescription medicines, but I encourage you to pray about trying some of the newer natural treatments.

The herb kava can relieve the tension-type headache, while migraines are best treated with feverfew or ginkgo biloba. Seek God about what you can do in the natural for your headaches, and believe Him to do the supernatural to bring about the manifestation of your healing.

A Prayer for Relief from Headaches

I come to You, Father, in the name of Jesus, seeking a manifestation of the healing that was purchased for me by Your Son two thousand years ago. Give me wisdom, knowledge, and insight about the headaches I am experiencing and reveal to me the type of headache and specifically the things that I should do in the natural to overcome this attack. I speak to the muscles in my neck, temple, and scalp area and command them, in the name of Jesus, to relax. I take authority over all of the stress and tension in these muscle groups. Direct me, Father, as to whether I should use an herbal treatment for these headaches. I further speak to the small arteries in my brain area, and I command the smooth muscle tone to be normal with no constriction or dilation in these vessels that would cause migraine pain. Again, direct me, Father, as to the use of feverfew and other natural treatments that will maintain the normal tone in these vessels. As I use these natural treatments, Father, I send forth Your anointing into them and command them to work according to Your perfect design. I thank You, Father, that the fear of tumors in my brain or the fear of going blind is driven out from my mind and I will walk in divine health. If my doctor recommends a prescription medicine, give me wisdom and insight as to whether to use this medicine as part of my pathway to healing. I thank You, Father, that in Jesus' name I can break the generational and genetic curse of headaches, and I declare that I will be set free of these. Thank You, Father, for Your touch today. And thank You, Lord, that the attack of headaches will not hinder me in completing the call and assignment upon my life. I praise You, Father, for all of Your healing provisions and most of all, for the name above all names that overcomes all the works of the enemy. In Jesus' name, I present these prayers and petitions before You. Amen.

SKIN DISEASES

Our skin is being subjected to increasing attacks from our environment. The treatment of skin disorders represents a major percentage of expenditures on health care. We have also seen that God has provided numerous avenues of protection to help us avoid and prevent a wide spectrum of skin diseases ranging from simple age-related changes to skin cancer.

Selenium, vitamin C, and vitamin E, along with extra omega-3 fatty acids (fish oils) are important for skin health. Selenium and vitamin E offer protection from the most common skin cancers, basal and squamous cell carcinomas. Biotin and grape seed extract also promote healthy skin, nails, and hair. All of these natural substances can be taken in a daily nutrient supplement and should be considered along with a healthy Mediterranean-style diet. Eating properly and taking a comprehensive nutritional supplement are the beginning steps in preserving and protecting us from skin problems.

A Prayer for Protection from Skin Diseases

Father, I thank You in the name of Jesus for healthy skin. I thank You, Father, for the revelation of natural substances from Your plant and animal kingdom that You have provided to me to protect my skin. I thank You that my skin will secrete the proper amounts of oil to keep the skin surface lubricated. I thank You, Father, for the supplements You have provided to support my underlying skin structure. I pray for wisdom and direction in utilizing supplements to my diet to reverse age-related changes and maintain healthy skin. Thank You, Father, that abnormal cell divisions in my skin that would result in skin cancers will not occur. I thank You for the natural substances I can use to protect myself from skin cancers. Thank You, Father, that as I utilize these various substances and do what I can do in the natural, You will place Your supernatural hand of protection upon my body. I thank You that right now, as I lay my hands upon my body, that if there are any abnormal cells they will wither and die. My confession is that no skin malignancy will exist in this temple. Thank You, Father, for Your divine protection and provision in this vital area of my body. In Jesus' name I pray, amen.

DIZZINESS

Dizziness is one of the most common neurological symptoms encountered in medical practice. The most common form of dizziness is known as *vertigo*. This term describes a sensation of motion when there is no motion, or an exaggerated sense of motion in response to certain body movements.

To maintain our balance, God created a complex series of organs that interact with each other. Poor circulation to the brain can cause dizziness, as can certain viral or bacterial infections. Abnormally high or low blood pressure and brain tumors are also causes of dizziness.

Due to inadequate oxygen supply to various organs, anemia can result in dizziness as well. One of the most common forms of vertigo is called "benign positional vertigo." This is a spinning sensation that is associated with changes in head position, particularly when suddenly sitting up or standing from a lying position. This form of vertigo tends to be brief and episodic, whereas viral or bacterial infections can cause an almost constant vertigo for several days and then disappear as the body's immune system functions take over.

As we get older, small amounts of debris can accumulate in the canals of the inner ear and activate tiny hair cells, resulting in false signals. Also, small crystals sometimes are mispositioned within the canals, resulting in false signals.

Any kind of persistent vertigo or dizziness should be evaluated by a physician to be certain there is not a more serious problem.

God has provided several natural nutrients that can help us with dizziness. For example, 100 mg of vitamin B_3 (niacin) three times daily can be very useful in stopping the dizziness because of its effect on cerebral circulation. This dosage should not be taken by a person with high blood pressure or a liver problem.

All of the B vitamins are important for normal brain and nervous system function. Taking water-soluble B vitamins as part of your daily nutrient supplement is critical in maintaining a healthy nervous system.

Extra B complex, 100 mg two to three times daily, as well as extra B_6, 50 mg daily, may be helpful during periods of dizziness. Up to 1,000 mcg of vitamin B_{12} daily can also be useful. I recommend vitamin C, 2,000 mg daily, and vitamin E, 800 IU (natural form) daily. Coenzyme Q_{10}, 90 to 150 mg daily, can be useful during periods of dizziness as well.

Certain herbs such as powdered whole gingerroot in doses of 500 to 1,000 mg can relieve dizziness and nausea. Ginkgo extract, 120 mg daily, helps to improve blood circulation to the brain. Patients with persistent vertigo might try meclizine (which is available over the counter), 25 to 50 mg every six hours.

Remember God's promise. If we would diligently hearken to His voice, He would allow none of the diseases on us that He allowed on the world (Ex. 15:26). If you are experiencing a problem with sudden vertigo or dizziness, you should pray about your specific pathway to healing. Let the Holy Spirit guide you and give you wisdom. In addition, you now have many God-created natural options from the plant kingdom to utilize against this attack.

A Prayer for Relief from Dizziness

Father, as I come before You in the name of Jesus, I give thanks to You for this fearfully and wonderfully created temple. Thank You, Father, that as I understand the attacks of the evil one against my body, all fear is cast on You, and I can pray and stand in faith against the attack of dizziness. I thank You, Father, that the circulation to my brain is normal. I also thank You, Father, for a strong, activated immune system that will arise and overcome any virus or bacteria that would attack my balance.

I thank You, Father, that my inner ear is normal and there will be no abnormal fluid accumulation or abnormal crystal deposits that would interfere with my balance.

I thank You, Father, that the symptoms of vertigo and dizziness must go in Jesus' name, and my brain will receive normal signals to overcome the dizziness.

I further speak to all the nutrients You have provided, Father, and I command Your anointing to flow through these natural substances to bring healing to my body. Guide me, Lord, through the Holy Spirit, the One who guides me to all truth, as to the specific things in the natural that I should do.

As I pray over the natural substances, let Your peace guide me to all truth and reveal those things that would most benefit me. Alert me, Father, as to whether I need further tests or consultation with a physician. I set myself in agreement with Your Word that my recovery will be speedy. I trust, Father, that as I do all that I can and know to do in the natural, You will perform the supernatural to relieve me of these symptoms in my body. Thank You for this revelation knowledge. Thank You for the anointing that resides within me. In the name of Jesus I give You praise and thanks. Amen.

VEIN PROBLEMS

Varicose veins and chronic venous insufficiency are common problems affecting up to 15 percent of men and 25 percent of women. Though the symptoms are often simply very annoying (leg swelling, skin changes, itching, etc.), in some cases venous problems can be life-threatening, particularly if blood clots form in the veins that are not functioning properly. A consistent principle of God's healing is that there is a unique pathway to healing for each individual. This may be a supernatural, miraculous manifestation of healing, but it is often the supernatural power of our prayers and authority as believers combined with the natural treatments that God has provided to heal our bodies. One such natural treatment is from an herb. Scientific studies show that an herbal extract from the seed of the horse chestnut tree can improve venous circulation and increase the tone of veins, preventing leakage of fluid, swelling, and pain in the extremities.

If you or a loved one is suffering from venous problems in the lower extremities (and almost all of us know someone who is), please consider carefully this prayer and share it with others.

A PRAYER FOR HEALING OF VARICOSE VEINS

Father, I come to You in the precious name of my Lord and Savior, Jesus. I thank You that He bore my infirmities on the cross two thousand years ago, and by His stripes I was healed. By the authority in that name, I speak to the veins in my extremities, and I command the valves in those veins to function normally. I command the pressure in the veins and capillaries to decrease and the fluid leaking from those vessels to decrease and disappear. Furthermore, I take authority over the formation of any blood clot that might form in those veins and I say that my blood flow will be normal in Jesus' name. I pray specifically for the Holy Spirit to guide me to the truth of my pathway to healing. If I am to use a natural treatment, I pray that Your anointing will flow through this seed extract and those chemicals that You created within this extract will begin healing my veins. As I do the things in the natural that I have received knowledge of, I will trust You, Father, to do the supernatural that I cannot do. Thank You, Lord, for Your hand of protection upon me, and I thank You that the full manifestation of healing is mine. I praise You, Father, for these things. In Jesus' name, amen.

HIP PROBLEMS

Over a quarter of a million people each year require total hip joint replacement due to the degeneration of hip cartilage as a result of "wear-and-tear" arthritis (osteoarthritis). Each time you take a step, sixty-two different bones are moved, but it is the hip joint that must absorb tremendous weight-bearing pressures. This can literally destroy cartilage. Certain natural substances such as glucosamine, 1,500 mg daily, can help reduce pain and restore cartilage loss. The enemy desires to hinder and attack God's children by causing destruction of this joint, and we must do all we can in the natural to protect our joints.

We must also apply sound, spiritual principles so that we can speak to our body and command a hedge of protection over the cartilage and bones of the joint. If you have noticed symptoms of pain in your hip, get more information about the nature of the attack so that you will know how to pray.

Paul wrote that we should not be unaware of the schemes or devices of the enemy. If for no other reason, having our hip joints checked provides us a specific avenue for prayer. The disciples of Jesus said to Him, "Lord, teach us to pray" (Luke 11:1).

We must realize that there are specific ways to pray that enable our prayers to be most effective. I have prayed the following prayer for patients with hip problems. I encourage you to review this prayer and to believe God to intervene in your situation.

A Prayer for Healing of Hip Problems

Father, in the name of Jesus, I thank You for the wonderful design You created in my hip joint. I thank You, Father, that this joint was designed to be pain-free and last throughout my lifetime. I thank You for the strong cartilage lining that enables the joint to work properly, and I thank You for the fluid that lubricates the surface of this joint. In the name of Jesus, I speak to any roughness or irregularities in the cartilage and command any thinning or deterioration of the cartilage in my hip joint to be restored to normal. I speak to the fluid and command it to be in ample supply. Guide me, Father, in the things I can do to protect and restore my hip joint. Reveal to me the proper amount of exercise I need to do, and reveal to me specific natural treatments such as glucosamine to restore and protect the cartilage of my joint. I speak Your anointing through glucosamine, chondroitin, and any other natural substance or method You would instruct me to use to take care of this precious and vital part of my temple. Thank You, Father, that I will continue to be a light to the world around me and that I will be able to stand, sit, and walk normally—clear of pain, stiffness, and limitation of movement in my hip joint. I thank You for all of these things, Father, in the name of Jesus. Thank You that as I do what I know to do in the natural, You will do the supernatural that I cannot do. In Jesus' name, I present this petition before You. Amen.

CHRONIC FATIGUE SYNDROME

C hronic fatigue syndrome (CFS) has become a vexing problem for both patients and doctors alike. The exact cause of this debilitating syndrome characterized by extreme fatigue is not known, but current research seems to indicate that an overreactivity of the body's immune system is involved. Many patients can trace the onset of the severe fatigue to an infection such as a cold or flu, a stressful event such as an accident, or an unusually stressful situation in their lives. At these times, the body's immune system function is stimulated; but after the viral or bacterial infection or other stressful event is over, the body's immune system, for reasons not known, stays activated. We have found that working with patients to balance the immune system is one of the more effective ways in the natural to deal with CFS.

It has recently been discovered also that this immune system imbalance can affect a key chemical in the body known as ATP (adenosine triphosphate). ATP provides the body with energy, thus affecting muscle strength and, in general, increases energy production within cells. A study in *Annals of Allergy, Asthma, and Immunology* related research on an over-the-counter food-derived nutritional supplement known as nicotinamide adenine dinucleotide (NAD). Patients taking 10 mg daily reported a marked improvement in their symptoms of chronic fatigue syndrome. The supplement proved to have no major side effects.

Based on these facts, we can pray an effectual, fervent prayer for healing of chronic fatigue syndrome. Here is a prayer that we often pray with our patients. It might be helpful to you as you come before the throne of God seeking your healing from chronic fatigue syndrome.

A Prayer for Healing
of Chronic Fatigue Syndrome

Father, I come to You in the name of Jesus, thanking You that Jesus bore in His own body on the cross two thousand years ago the infirmity of chronic fatigue syndrome that has attacked my body. I therefore pray, Father, that You will guide me to the pathway that will lead to the total manifestation of my healing. In the name of Jesus, I speak to my immune system and I command it to become balanced according to the Word of God and according to the way You created it to function. I speak to any abnormal chemical levels in my body and command them to also become normal. I command the ATP levels that produce energy in my body to become normal in Jesus' name. I thank You, Father, that as I do my part and balance my immune system with the natural substances You created, You will supernaturally touch and heal me of this attack of darkness. I thank You, Lord, for revelation knowledge of new chemicals discovered in Your creation that will help set me free. Thank You, Father, that there is a unique pathway for me to walk on, and as I am obedient and go my way I will be set free and will be satisfied with long life on this earth according to Your promise. In Jesus' name, I thank You that my healing manifestation is coming, and through my eye of faith, I see myself healed. Amen.

LUPUS

Lupus (medically known as SLE or systemic lupus erythematosus) is actually a disorder of the body's immune system in which components of the immune system attack multiple organs in the body. It is therefore called an "auto-immune disorder." Eighty-five percent of patients with lupus are women, and it is felt that estrogen may play a role in this disease since most cases develop after menarche and before menopause. Lupus occurs in one of every 1,000 white women and in one of every 250 black women. There is a genetic component to the disease as it can occur in families. Certain types of drugs can also cause a form of lupus.

The symptoms that occur with lupus are caused by the components of the immune system that attack the eyes and the lining of joints, as well as the heart muscle and lining of the heart. Inflammation of the lining of blood vessels can cause abdominal pain, colon problems, and inflammation of the kidneys, spleen, and thyroid gland also occur. In praying for and standing against lupus, it is important to break the generational curse (genetic tendency) according to Deuteronomy 5:9: "Thou shalt not bow down thyself unto them, nor serve them: for I the LORD thy God am a jealous God, visiting the iniquity of the fathers upon the children unto the third and fourth generation of them that hate me." First, the generational curse must be broken over yourself and over any future generations of your offspring that could have this genetic trait passed on to them. Second, it is important to speak directly to an over-reactive, oversensitized immune system that is mistakenly attacking components of your own body.

The mountain (an overreactive, oversensitized immune system) needs to be removed by the healing power of God according to Mark 11:23.

A Prayer for Healing of Lupus

Father, I come before You in the mighty name of Jesus. I thank You, Father, that Your Son, Jesus, bore in His own body two thousand years ago on Calvary the disease of lupus. I therefore thank You that by His stripes I was healed, and I therefore come before You seeking the full manifestation of total and complete healing from lupus. I speak, Father, in the name of Jesus to the components of my immune system that are mistakenly attacking my own body, and I command my immune system to recognize the normal components in my body. I speak balance to the immune cells and protection over my heart, lungs, joints, kidneys, and every cell, organ, and blood vessel in my body. I ask You, Father, to show me the specific pathway that will lead to total healing in my body.

Reveal through the leading of the Holy Spirit those natural substances that I can take to balance my immune system, and as I do all that I can do in the natural, Father, I look to You to do the supernatural to produce the full manifestation of healing in my temple. I thank You, Father, that according to 1 Peter 2:24 I was healed, and I thank You that the full, complete, and total manifestation of that healing is mine. Through my eye of faith I see myself healed. I thank You, Father, for this healing manifestation in the precious name of Jesus. Amen.

LOW BACK PAIN

Low back pain is one of the most commonly encountered problems physicians and patients face. There are a variety of causes, but most cases of low back pain will clear up on their own. However, there are certain things that we need to do. Years ago the recommended treatment was for patients to remain flat on their backs in bed for two to three weeks, but this has changed dramatically.

A presentation by Gary E. Ruoff, M.D., at the 51st Annual Assembly of the American Academy of Family Physicians, summarized some of the latest treatments that are most effective for back problems. The "flat on your back for several weeks" has now been reduced to no more than two days of bed rest and then to begin a mild exercise program. Exercising for fifteen minutes twice daily (involving stretching and light walking) for three days weekly is ideal. Even if back pain is due to a disk that is herniated (which a doctor can often tell by simply tapping reflexes at the knee and ankle and having the patient raise the big toe!), exercise will solve 90 percent of the problem.

The researcher pointed out that if a patient is *sitting* in the exam room with a rigid back, the back pain is usually muscle strain, whereas if the patient is *standing,* it's more likely to be a herniated disk. Patients with spinal stenosis (a narrowing of the spinal canal) can often walk uphill but have problems with pain when walking downhill. Back pain can also be caused by infection, and there are specific ways to test for this involving something as simple as tapping over the spine.

Osteoarthritis is one of the most common causes of back pain, which usually begins around age fifty, and herniated disks are seen more frequently in the thirty- to fifty-year-old age-group. Doctors are now changing their thinking and feel that it is better to manage back pain with minimal drugs. Often 85 to 90 percent of the cases go away on their own, but 10 to 15 percent of patients do have a significant problem. Either of the new nonirritating, anti-inflammatory prescription drugs (Celebrex or Vioxx) is very safe and effective for back pain. Muscle relaxants are useful mainly for muscle spasms. Also, many patients notice relief with chiropractic or osteopathic manipulation or massage therapy, but this is short-term relief and patients must be transitioned into an exercise program. Exercise is critical because it literally builds a "muscle cast" to hold the spine in place. A physical therapist is an ideal medical resource to give specific advice on back exercise. If the only exercise a patient can do is walking, this will work.

A Prayer for Healing of Low Back Pain

Father, I thank You in Jesus' name that I have been healed of this back pain by the stripes of Jesus two thousand years ago. I am praying, therefore, for the total and complete manifestation of healing of this pain, believing that as healing is manifested, I will not face this pain anymore. I ask You, Father, to show me the specific pathway that will lead to healing of this pain. If there are anti-inflammatory agents that I should be on for a period of time, alert me through the Holy Spirit to this. Reveal to me the proper exercise I should do and give me the strength in my flesh to pursue this. I thank You, Father, that there will be no nerve damage, that I will never require surgery, and that the pain, whether it be muscular or due to nerve impingement, will cease completely. As the manifestation of my physical healing occurs, I will use this temple to complete "the course You have called me to finish" on this earth to touch the lives of others. Thank You, Father, that I was healed, and through my eye of faith I see my healing manifest. In Jesus' name, amen.

ESOPHAGEAL PROBLEMS

I sn't it just like the enemy to have us think that recurring episodes of heartburn are nothing more than a minor annoyance? Most of the time this is the case. However, we must be on guard not to open the door to potentially serious problems in the lower esophagus, which transports food into the stomach.

The culprit in heartburn and esophageal acid reflux is often a weak muscular valve between the stomach and esophagus. Peppermint candy, coffee, and chocolate all weaken this valve, allowing acid to irritate the lower esophagus. Eating large meals late at night and being overweight increase this acid reflux. Chronic irritation of the esophagus may just be an aggravation, but in some cases, it can lead to cancerous changes in the cells of the esophagus.

If you are experiencing heartburn and acid reflux, you need to take authority and pray an "effectual fervent prayer," according to James 5:16.

A Prayer for Healing and Protection
from Esophageal Problems

Father, I come to You in the name that is above all names, the name of Jesus. I thank You that as a child of God, the Holy Spirit dwells in me and guides me to all truth. Therefore, in the name of Jesus, I ask You to alert me to any potential damage or problem in my esophagus.

I speak to the valve between my esophagus and my stomach and command it to have normal muscle tone and protect my esophagus from acid reflux. I speak to all the cells lining my esophagus and command them to be normal and not to be affected by any foreign acid.

Alert me, Father, to the things that I can and should do in the natural to protect this vital area of my temple and alert me to any potential danger. I thank You that I was healed by the stripes of Jesus and therefore I am healed right now. As I do all that I can and know to do in the natural, I will trust You, Father, to do the supernatural.

Thank You, Father, that You care so much about me that You would alert me in this area of my body. In the mighty name of Jesus I pray, amen.

DIGESTIVE DISEASES

I t's a tube about thirty or so feet long, but when it doesn't function properly, you can get into big problems. We're talking about the digestive tract, which doctors generally call the gastrointestinal (GI) tract. This tube digests food, absorbs water, secretes important enzymes, and essentially keeps us alive and keeps our bodies healthy.

It starts at the mouth and ends at the anal opening (I know you don't like to talk about this, but God created it). It takes food from as little as twenty hours to as long as three or four days to pass through this muscular tube. Digestion actually begins in the mouth as enzymes are secreted in the saliva and chemically break down food that our teeth have already mechanically broken down.

Food quickly passes into the throat or pharynx area in just a few seconds and then into the esophagus. The esophagus is around ten inches long, more or less, and food takes half a minute or up to a minute to get through it; with liquids it takes only a few seconds. There is a small, one-way valve between the esophagus and the stomach that directs food into the stomach only and prevents stomach acid from returning to the esophagus.

As food gets into the stomach, it is mixed with gastric juices and hydrochloric acid, which are designed to destroy various bacteria and other organisms that might be present in food. Food will usually remain in the stomach approximately four hours, but can stay up to six or seven hours if you have eaten large amounts of fatty foods. This is why eating a large fatty meal late at night causes food to "sit in your stomach" for hours and can cause a lot of misery.

From the stomach food passes into the small intestine. Various secretions enable the small intestine and the large intestine to absorb food properly. Most digestive processes and food absorption into the body takes place in the small intestine. As we get older, we do not produce as many of these enzymes, and a daily nutritional supplement containing digestive enzymes is very helpful.

After leaving the small intestine, digested food passes into the colon or large intestine. By this time most of the nutrients have been absorbed, except sodium and other salts, which are taken into the body in the colon. The remainder of the nonabsorbed food is formed into stool, and water is taken from the remainder of the food residue and absorbed. It takes about fourteen hours for these processes to take place in the colon.

God has created a wonderful system that usually functions flawlessly. We can, however, do certain things such as add digestive enzymes (amylase, protease, lipase, cellulase, lactase, and others) to help supplement the loss of enzymes as we get older. Other substances such as cinnamon bark, fennel seed, and peppermint leaf powder are helpful in maintaining our digestion and proper absorption of nutrients.

We all face potential attacks against our GI tract as we get older. But by taking natural supplements, timing our meals properly (that is, not eating late in the evening), and eating sufficient quantities of soluble and insoluble fiber, we can protect ourselves from most digestive problems.

By studying what the various areas of the GI tract do, we can take authority and pray effectively to prevent and overcome many common diseases.

A Prayer for Protection
from Digestive Diseases

Father, I come to You in the name of Jesus, thanking You for the fearful and wonderful design of my body. I thank You for a healthy digestive system that will properly absorb the nutrients You created to bring health to my body. I pray specifically for healthy teeth, gums, and bone structure in my mouth to begin the digestion of my food. I thank You that my esophagus will contract normally, and I thank You that the valve will close properly at the end of my esophagus to prevent heartburn and scarring from stomach acid.

I thank You that my stomach will secrete proper amounts of acid and enzymes and that it will be free of bacteria that might cause peptic ulcer disease. Thank You that the valve that empties my stomach will function properly, preventing food from backing up in my stomach area. I thank You that I will secrete the proper amounts of enzymes into my small intestine to digest and absorb food. I thank You for a healthy gallbladder that secretes bile and a healthy pancreas that secretes enzymes. Thank You that my food will be absorbed as it passes through my system, and I thank You for a healthy colon and healthy cells in my colon that will remain free of abnormal cell divisions that could cause polyps or cancer. I praise You that I will be free of pockets in my colon that might become inflamed and that I will remain free of diverticulitis. Thank You for providing the knowledge of supplemental enzymes, and give me wisdom to consume these, along with proper amounts of fiber and proper timing of my meals, to protect my digestive tract. In Jesus' name, I call myself free of digestive problems and diseases. As I do all I can and know to do in the natural, I will trust and look to You, Father, to do all that I cannot do. In Jesus' name I pray. Amen.

JOURNAL PAGES

Journal pages can be very important in the process of healing. The Bible says in Philippians 4:6 to "present our prayers and petitions before God." There is something about writing theses prayers down and recording the specific date you presented your petitions before God that strengthens your faith for healing.

Use these pages for your prayers, either for yourself or for a friend or loved one. Be specific. Pray without ceasing. Then trust God for the healing manifestation.

NAME: _____

DATE: _____

HEALTH CHALLENGE: _____

_____

_____

_____

MY PRAYER FOR HEALING: _____

_____

_____

MY PRAYER ANSWERED: _____

_____

_____

WHEN: _____

HOW GOD HEALED: _____

_____

NAME: _____

DATE: _____

HEALTH CHALLENGE: _____

_____

_____

_____

MY PRAYER FOR HEALING: _____

_____

_____

MY PRAYER ANSWERED: _____

_____

_____

WHEN: _____

HOW GOD HEALED: _____

_____

NAME: _____

DATE: _____

HEALTH CHALLENGE: _____

_____

_____

_____

MY PRAYER FOR HEALING: _____

_____

_____

MY PRAYER ANSWERED: _____

_____

_____

WHEN: _____

HOW GOD HEALED: _____

_____

NAME: _____

DATE: _____

HEALTH CHALLENGE: _____

_____

_____

_____

MY PRAYER FOR HEALING: _____

_____

_____

MY PRAYER ANSWERED: _____

_____

_____

WHEN: _____

HOW GOD HEALED: _____

_____

NAME: _____

DATE: _____

HEALTH CHALLENGE: _____

_____

_____

_____

MY PRAYER FOR HEALING: _____

_____

_____

MY PRAYER ANSWERED: _____

_____

_____

WHEN: _____

HOW GOD HEALED: _____

_____

NAME: _____

DATE: _____

HEALTH CHALLENGE: _____

_____

_____

_____

MY PRAYER FOR HEALING: _____

_____

_____

MY PRAYER ANSWERED: _____

_____

_____

WHEN: _____

HOW GOD HEALED: _____

_____

NAME: _____

DATE: _____

HEALTH CHALLENGE: _____

_____

_____

_____

MY PRAYER FOR HEALING: _____

_____

_____

MY PRAYER ANSWERED: _____

_____

_____

WHEN: _____

HOW GOD HEALED: _____

_____

NAME: _____

DATE: _____

HEALTH CHALLENGE: _____

_____

_____

_____

MY PRAYER FOR HEALING: _____

_____

_____

MY PRAYER ANSWERED: _____

_____

_____

WHEN: _____

HOW GOD HEALED: _____

_____

NAME: _____

DATE: _____

HEALTH CHALLENGE: _____
_____
_____
_____

MY PRAYER FOR HEALING: _____
_____
_____

MY PRAYER ANSWERED: _____
_____
_____

WHEN: _____

HOW GOD HEALED: _____
_____

Name: _____

Date: _____

Health Challenge: _____

_____

_____

_____

My Prayer for Healing: _____

_____

_____

My Prayer Answered: _____

_____

_____

When: _____

How God Healed: _____

_____

DR. REGINALD CHERRY has been in the practice of preventive medicine for over twenty-five years. An ordained minister as well as a physician, Dr. Cherry has expanded his outreach to help more people through Reginald B. Cherry Ministries. His weekly television program *The Doctor and the Word* reaches eighty million households. He teaches about natural treatments combined with God's Word and the power of prayer. He also publishes a monthly medical newsletter and has published numerous books, two of which made the bestsellers list. His goal is to help people find their "pathway to healing" according to John 9:7.